Golf & the Abundant Life

Daniel A. Tomlinson, M.D.

YorkshirePublishing
www.yorkshirepublishing.com
Write Now

Dedication

Dedicated to Omer "Spike" Tomlinson.
My father and the man who taught me the game I love.

Table of Contents

Introduction .... *vii*

Keep Your Eye on the Ball 1
Less is More 5
Tempo 9
Good Bounces 13
Bad Bounces.. 17
Taking the Low Percentage Shot 21
Course Knowledge 25
Iron Sharpens Iron 29
Trusting the Line 33
Preparation 35
Practice 39
Playing By the Rules 43
Helping a Friend Find His Lost Ball......................47
Finding a Friend's Lost Ball 51
The Sandie..55

Epilogue *59*

About the Author *61*

Acknowledgements *63*

Introduction

I was nine years of age when Dad first took me golfing. He was a war hero in the Pacific theater during WWII. Saved many members of his Marine platoon in the battle of Okinawa. I idolized him! He was bigger than life to me. So when he invited me to tag along with his golfing buddies, well, it was truly something special. How would I not fall in love with the game!

That was 1964. I've been enjoying the game ever since. It indeed, is a game for life. Basketball, baseball and water skiing have had to be dropped with aging. Skiing & snowboarding are done much more cautiously, but golf, not so. It's the only game that I'm better at now, than when I was young! You see, golf imitates life, and more specifically, golf imitates spiritual life. Many of the secrets of good golf are also the secrets to a good life, to a godly life!

I know this because besides Dr. Dan Tomlinson the golf guy, I'm Dr. Dan Tomlinson the Bible guy. I can't remember when I didn't love God & his Son Jesus, but I can remember when I started taking God's Word seriously. It was March 9th 1973 as a senior at Shawnee Mission South High School. A school mate gave me a copy of the Campus Crusade's well-known, Four Spiritual Laws. You may remember; #1. God loves you and has a plan for your life. #2. Your sin has unfortunately separated you from him, creating a great chasm between you & God. #3. Jesus Christ has bridged that chasm by his atoning sacrifice on the Cross of Calvary for you. #4. All you must do to receive the free gift of salvation he offers is to repent of your sins & ask him to be your Savior. Well, something clicked that day and I went from thinking I was heading to Hell because of my sin & stupidity to knowing I was destined for Heaven to be with Jesus someday. What a revelation that was! I became interested in the Bible and read it often from that day forward.

In the Bible are secrets for life. For the Bible reveals who is our Lord and he has a name. It's Jesus & he is the truth that sets you & me free.

> Then said Jesus to those Jews which believed on him. If you continue in my word, then you are my disciples indeed; and you shall know the truth and the truth shall make you free.
>
> John 8:31-32

Pilate asked Jesus on that fateful day, "What is truth?" (John 18:38). Not realizing He was standing in its presence! For indeed truth is that which is aligned with the character, mind, will & glory of God.

Jesus said that He has come to give life and that more abundantly, (John 10:10). So in getting to know my Lord through His Word, I have learned much truth. As the psalmist penned, "I understand more than the ancients, because I keep thy precepts" (Psalm 119:100). I have been given insight into the character, mind, will & glory of God. And a funny thing happened, in studying the Bible and in playing golf, I began to notice many similarities, many parallels, between successful living and successful golfing. For indeed, golf is a spiritual game. Jesus said, he who dies shall live, good golfing says, less is more, it's not how hard you hit it but it's how good you hit it! Jesus said, follow me, good golfing says, keep your eye on the ball. The

Bible says, in this world you shall suffer tribulation, every golfer knows that sometimes a good shot will take a bad bounce. And on & on it goes. Golf and life. Two peas in the same pod. Lot's to think about.

Of course, I'm not the first one to notice these parallels. As a young man I remember reading the wonderful British book entitled *Golf in the Kingdom* by Michael Murphy. What a mystical journey that was. I can recall incorporating much of what I learned in calming myself to play better golf. Then of course, *Harvey Penick's Little Red Book* was published. Limericks like "take dead aim" & "the magic move" became part of many of our golfing vocabularies as we sought to emulate that master teacher's Zen. More recently, David Cook's book, *Golf's Sacred Journey; Seven Days at the Links of Utopia* taught me that the rhythm, balance & tempo of fly fishing (as the object lesson) has everything to do with the proper golf swing.

For indeed, golf, like life, is a head game. As has been said about life by author-pastor Joyce Meyers, "the battlefield is the mind." So too, when asked by others what my handicap is, I often respond, "my handicap, well, it's between my ears!"

So let's look at some golf tips and see how they can both, make us better golfers & better people. People well fit for the Master's use & good pleasure.

> Thou art worthy O Lord to receive glory, honor
> & power, for thou has created all things, and for
> your pleasure they were & are created.

REVELATION 4:11

Keep Your Eye on the Ball

There are many distractions in the golf swing that can interfere with the success of the shot. When I think about where my club is at the top or worry about my takeaway, when I'm thinking about my balance or my tempo during the swing I am destined to miss-hit the ball. Indeed, it's only when I keep my eye on the ball during the swing and concentrate on getting the club on the ball at the proper angle and inclination that success occurs.

So it is in spiritual life. The Bible tells me that I am to set my eyes on the Lord in order to have success in this life.

> Looking unto Jesus the author and finisher of
> our faith;

Hebrews 12:2

You see, Jesus is the author of my faith. The Word of God states clearly that he is the way, the truth and the life (John 14:6). He is the one pictured by the Passover Lamb in the Old Testament as causing the angel of death to pass over the children of Israel. He is our substitute. He became sin for us, so that we may become the righteousness of God in him (II Corinthians 5:21). Isaiah proclaimed that upon him was laid the iniquity of us all (Isaiah 53:6). Without Jesus and his atoning sacrifice, faith by itself is useless. As the Paul stated in his letter to the Corinthians, if Christ be not risen from the dead, our faith is in vain, we are still in our sins & we are of all men most miserable (I Corinthians 15:17-19). Faith in our leaders, in the economy, in our own strength, abilities & health won't deliver in the day of trouble. Faith in philosophy, education, religion or enlightenment won't see me through when I'm on my death bed and peering over the precipice of eternity. Of course, the reason faith in those things won't save is that philosophy, education, religion & enlightenment did not rise from the dead. Only Jesus defeated death, only he is the One who can deliver on the promise to do that for you & me too. Indeed, truth & faith are married in belief in the Lord Jesus Christ.

So when I look to Jesus, things go well in this life. Psalm 73 states it well;

> Nevertheless I am continually with thee: Thou hast held me by my right hand. Thou shalt guide me with thy counsel, and afterward receive me to glory.

> PSALM 73:23-24

I think of Peter on that stormy night out on the Sea of Galilee. Remember when he and the disciples saw Jesus walking on the water towards them. They weren't sure if they were seeing reality or a ghost. Yet Jesus told them to fear not, for it was indeed he. To that Peter said, "Lord if it is you, bid me to come out to you." Jesus said "come." And lo & behold, Peter did just that. He walked on water as he kept his eyes on Jesus. But then, he, like we all can do, looked away. He noticed the waves and the wind, and down he went. He sank back into the water only to be rescued by his Lord & helped back into the boat.

That's the way it is for me too. In the morning I can start out so good. I may spend a bit of time reading in the Bible &

praying for people. I'm ready to go out and make a difference. Then, life intervenes. Problems at work, a situation at home, whatever it is can cause my puny mind to look away from my source of strength & refreshment. And you know what happens next, I miss the mark!

In golf, the same thing can happen. I can warm up on the range, swinging easy and getting into a good frame of mind for the upcoming round. I may even par the first few holes as I'm hitting well struck shots keeping my eye on the ball. But soon, little thoughts start creeping in. Is my left elbow straight? Is my takeaway low enough? Is my swing plane correct? And just like Peter, I start to sink as I forget to keep my eye on the ball. The antidote of course, is to do what the big fisherman did. He put his eyes back on the Lord. When I mess up in my day or when I start miss-hitting the ball, I need to refocus back to the center. Refocus back on the ball, refocus back on the Lord.

Really, as I think about a golf round. There is always going to be some problem times. Part of becoming a good player is learning how to handle adversity and developing the ability to fix a problem during the round. That's true for life too, isn't it. Bouncing back, when I hit a rough patch is the mark of a healthy soul. And looking to Jesus is always the best way to bounce back. Just ask Peter!

For Further Study:

1. What would be a good swing thought for you?
2. What would be a good thought to have when you first awaken in the morning? Would you consider Psalm 118:24 as a good first thought?
3. Jesus tells us in John 15 to abide in him. What does abiding in the Lord look like?

Less is More

Ben Hogan was quoted as saying about the golf swing, "it's not how hard you hit it, it's how good you hit it!" And that really is so true. When I'm lining up a shot that needs to carry the bunker or must pierce into the wind, I so often feel I should put some extra "mustard" on the swing in order to get the ball to the green. In reality though, as most golfers will agree, that is the worst thing I can do. Swinging too hard, nine times out of ten, leads to miss hits as one will sway back and hit behind the ball or accelerate too quickly and send the ball screaming to the left. Both mistakes leave me in more trouble than if I would have just swung easy, watched the ball go directly at the target and then either was rewarded with a chance at a one or two putt or dealt with a relatively easy sand shot over having to come back from the chili-dip miss-hit or my bad left-sided rocket.

The secret of overcoming this very natural swing tendency is to stop caring so much! That's right, it's not that big of a deal, and I need to realize that much of the fun of golf is negotiating the hazards and the good feeling that comes from that, but also it's fun to get out of the trouble with a good shot after finding myself in a tough spot. The other day I made a "double sandie." That's a par after hitting into two sand traps on the same hole. Boy, what a fun feeling it was to shoot out of that second bunker and one putt for a par!

Well in life the same things happens when I try too hard. It's a works mentality verses walking in the spirit. When I feel like

I have to work at doing the right thing, work at pleasing God, work at being a good person, I'm destined to fail. You see, it's by God's Spirit that I'm able to do anything of value. Jesus said it well in John 15 when he told his disciples, and by extension us, that he is the Vine and we are the branches. Apart from him we can do nothing. To amplify on the concept of the nothing that our Lord was speaking of, it means apart from him I can do nothing of any eternal value. That's why I need to walk in the spirit in life, go with the flow is another way of thinking of this concept. Listening to that still small voice that speaks to me and tells me to go to the left or the right would be another way of saying it.

One of my favorite verses illustrating this idea of walking in the Spirit is found in Psalms;

> Delight yourself in the Lord and he will give you
> the desires of your heart. Commit thy way unto
> the Lord; trust also in him, and he shall bring it
> to pass.

Psalm 37:4-5

Like Augustine has written, "love God with all your heart, soul & might, and then do whatever you want!" That's the secret, I don't want to work up my spirituality. It won't impress God, and it will only make me miserable. Again, it's like swinging too hard on that approach shot.

In comparing the works mentality to walking in the spirit, or swinging too hard verses going with the flow of the swing, Paul preaches accurately of our dilemma in Romans. In chapter seven he frankly speaks as he admits that he so often does what he does not want to do and doesn't do what he wants to do. He concludes his transparent talk by saying "Oh wretched man that

I am, who shall deliver me from the body of this death?" The answer, why it's found in the next verse. "I thank God through Jesus Christ our Lord. So then with the mind I myself serve the law of God; but with the flesh the law of sin" (Romans 7:24-25).

You see, Paul doesn't ask "what shall save me," but "who" shall save me from these dead tendencies that I have. He realizes it's in & through our Lord that we overcome. Not by extra effort & work. Again, same in golf. When I micromanage my swing, when I focus on all of the parts instead of feeling the process, I am destined for failure. It becomes the opposite of my desire and a bad shot is often the result.

Jesus spoke of living life in a way that may seem initially counter-intuitive but is nonetheless true when he said "If any man come after me, let him deny himself, take up his cross & follow me. For whosoever seeks to save his life shall lose it, but whosoever will lose his life for my sake shall find it" (Matthew 16:24). As I go my own way, I die. As I die to self and follow Him, I live. This is applicable in golf also. As I tense up over a shot worrying about how it will turn out I often fail in my shot making, but when I relax over that same shot, not really worrying about how it will turn out, then I hit the pure shot that I was desiring all along!

For Further Study:

1. What does losing your life for Jesus' sake mean to you?
2. Do you have a pre-swing thought over the ball to help you relax?
3. How do these two statements differ & is it important? "I have to keep God's law"…"I get to keep God's law."

Tempo

Everyone who teaches golf emphasizes the importance of correct tempo in the golf swing. It is taught that there is a certain relaxed flow to the swing which often results in proper ball-striking. Tempo is sort of hard to define but I think we all know it when we see it. The guy or gal, standing over the ball in balance, and then we witness a smooth takeaway followed by a relaxed transition to the downswing centered from the body's core, next we see the right arm drop into the "slot" which results in constant acceleration of the club into the ball for a nice shot. Truly, it's a thing of beauty!

Tempo is broken down into its components of balance and rhythm. These are easiest to define by thinking of their opposites. A golfer falling out of the swing after impact is certainly out of balance. A jerky transition from backswing to downswing is a swing without proper rhythm.

Life, like golf, needs to be lived in balance. I desire a flow in my day to day life that predictably leads me to succeed much like proper tempo helps me stay in the fairway from hole to hole verses hitting back & forth from one side of the fairway to the other.

Tucked away amidst so many gems in the fourth chapter of Paul's inspired words to the Philippians is a little statement that goes a long way towards maintaining balance in life.

> Let your moderation be known unto all men. The
> Lord is at hand.

PHILIPPIANS 4:5

Just like I yearn for a swing where other golfers can appreciate a smoothness & rhythm, I long for a life which witnesses a steadiness, a relaxation which others may desire to emulate. I don't want to be praising the Lord on Sunday morning and then be found complaining about the stock market or my health to others Sunday afternoon. Really, I want to be a positive person. I don't want to bring people down with complaining, negativity and especially by flagrant sin.

So how do I do this? (Remembering from our last chapter that the flesh so often will get in the way and derail my good intentions.) Look at the last little part of Philippians 4:5; "The Lord is at hand." This is good news! The Lord is in control. He has given me his spirit to dwell within. I can rejoice. I don't have to get worked up & anxious but I can just simply trust him. Psalm 131 says it oh so well;

> O Lord, my heart is not lifted up; my eyes are
> not raised too high; I do not occupy myself with
> things to great and too marvelous for me. But I
> have calmed and quieted my soul, like a weaned
> child with its mother; like a weaned child is my
> soul within me.

PSALM 131:1-2

KISS: "Keep is simple silly" is another way of thinking about this. I want to go with the flow of life, I want to keep the main thing the main thing. And I don't want to get bogged down with too much stuff. Of course, each of these little limericks has an application to the golf swing doesn't it? And I want to be calm. I wish to be like that child who is no longer pulling at my mother's clothes to get what I want. I want to be patient & still. When I'm standing over that 150 yard shot into the wind with the large sand trap in the front and to the right I long to be like that weaned child. I desire a calm & quieted soul!

Along with living life in moderation, I want to keep the main thing the main things as mentioned above. Paul's advice to his protégé Titus, speaks to how this is accomplished.

> For the grace of God that bringeth salvation hath appeared to all men. Teaching us that, denying ungodliness and worldly lusts, we should live soberly, righteously, and godly, in this present world: Looking for that blessed hope, and glorious appearing of the great God and our Savior Jesus Christ.
>
> TITUS 2:11-13

Living in moderation equates to not living in the world's ebb & flow. The lust of the flesh, the lust of the eyes & the pride of life will bring me down faster than I can say 1st John 2:16! I aspire to stay sober & in control as I walk in godliness & holiness. How do I do this? By living in the reality of the second part of these verses. As I look to the soon return of our great God & Savior my heart & mind are centered and put back into balance. Jesus is the main thing! It's not my finances, health or occupation. It's not even my family or my spouse, but it's knowing the Lord & making him known that brings balance to my life. That brings success in living.

As has been widely said, "If heaven is real, then it's all that matters; if heaven isn't real, then nothing matters at all." But heaven is real, God has set eternity in our hearts (Ecclesiastes 3:11), and as we live for heaven, realizing we are going to be with our wonderful Lord & Savior sooner than we realize, we can find balance & rhythm in our day to day lives.

For Further Study:

1. Where is your head in relation to the ball at the top of your backswing?
2. How long after you hit the ball does your left foot move out of place?
3. All successful businesses have a mission statement. Would "knowing Jesus & making him known" be a good mission statement for your life? Come up with one of your own.

Good Bounces

I was on the 6th hole yesterday at Running Y resort. Arnold Palmer designed it as a signature course for his power fade game. Located in the beautiful Klamath Basin, nestled below Crater Lake National Park and the Cascade mountain range, Running Y is an awesome place to spend the day golfing. Mountain, meadow & water vistas on every hole. Oh, and bald eagles flying often overhead adds to the enchantment.

So, there I was on the sixth, even par thus far and standing on the tee. The hole is lined by trees on both sides and sloped down toward the right. A big sand trap was out at 245 yards on the left and the green was 410 yards in the distance. So the plan I had committed myself to, was just as Arnie had designed this hole to be played. That is, aim toward the edge of the trap on the left and hit a slight fade envisioning the ball drifting right and rolling down the middle of the fairway toward the hole.

Well, that's not how the shot played out. I suppose because of the added distance for my sixty one year-old swing to propel the ball, I must have over swung a bit, coming "over-the-top" sending the ball curling left toward the pine trees on the edge of the relatively wide fairway. It was looking bad, probably going to go out of bounds into one of the nice vacation home yards which lined that particular hole. I was going to be teeing it up again with the two stroke disadvantage that comes with an out-of-bounds shot for sure. But then something wonderful and unexpected happened! My ball hit the trunk of the largest

Douglas fir tree, 220 yards away, at such an oblique angle that it knocked the ball to the right and forward another twenty yards. Rolling in the proper direction it stopped one yard short of the bunker with an excellent lie, ready for my next shot!

Most would call that luck, and indeed it was. But it's also a picture, an example if you will, of God's grace towards us. You see, we were all headed out-of-bounds. Our sin & stupidity had set our lives on a collision course with God's holy wrath. We were headed for destruction, we were headed for outer darkness. But then along came the tree of life, along came Jesus Christ. Jesus took my sins, became sin for you and me, and hung on that tree so that you & I could live with him & the Father, filled with his spirit, forever & ever! If that's not a good bounce, I don't know what is!

Good bounces in golf are called grace in life. G.R.A.C.E. God's Riches At Christ's Expense!

> For by grace are ye saved through faith; and that not of yourselves: It is the gift of God: Not of works, lest any man should boast.
>
> Ephesians 2:8-9

Grace has been called unmerited, unearned, undeserved favor. It is favor that should not have occurred, yet did. Like that good bounce, only multiplied a zillion times!

In golf we have a saying…"It's better to be lucky than good." But actually, both are best. Skill & luck are that winning combination that allows me to go low, well below my handicap occasionally. In life, grace travels with faith on a parallel track. They are intertwined for our success. As our verse in Ephesians states, it is by grace through faith that one is saved & made whole.

In the Book of Romans we learn additional insight about what faith offers.

> Therefore, being justified by faith, we have peace
> with God through our Lord Jesus Christ.

ROMANS 5:1

You see, peace in life comes from trusting God, not by having to figure everything out. God knows the future, I don't. When I worry about what is to come next, I lose my peace because I am not walking in faith. I am not trusting in God. One of Solomon's most quoted proverbs states it well;

> Trust in the Lord with all thine heart; and lean
> not unto thine own understanding. In all thy ways
> acknowledge him, and he shall direct thy paths.

PROVERBS 3:5-6

God, over & over in his Word, calls us to trust him, to walk in faith in order to receive the grace that he so abundantly bestows upon us. And that's because the price has been paid, we have been bought with a price. We have been adopted as sons & daughters into his family. And just like any mother or father, he is going to give good gifts, much mercy, and outrageous love to his kids.

> Let us therefore come boldly unto the throne of
> grace, that we may obtain mercy, and find grace
> to help in time of need.

HEBREWS 4:12

In the Old Testament, only the high priest, once a year, could come before God. But because of Christ, we who have embraced God's free gift of salvation by grace through faith in Jesus Christ, well, we can come boldly to our Papa anytime we desire just as that little toddler can run up and sit on daddy's lap, welcome & secure.

So, good bounces & skill, grace & faith. The winning formula in golf & in life!

For Further Study:

1. Have you had a good bounce in life because of God's grace to you? What was it?
2. Can Philippians 4:6-7 help you in times of worry?
3. Do you expect any luck to come your way when you golf? Why or why not?

Bad Bounces

Agood golf course is designed to have trouble spots along the way. Traps, trees, hills, lakes & hazards are part of the interest & intrigue of playing that favorite course. So, I shouldn't be surprised when an occasional good shot ends up in a bad place. In fact, I should expect that to occur in just about every round! How boring it is to visit that course where all of the holes are the same and no matter whether your shot was a good one or just mediocre, the outcome is the same. Sort of like reading a well written mystery book. There is always going to be tension & drama before the resolution, restitution & reward at the end. If not, no one would want to spend their time reading it.

So it is with our lives. God is writing a story and you and I are the main characters. And like that good novel, stuff is going to happen along the way. Imagine how dull your life would seem if every day were a "good day." To take this thought further, if every day were a good day, well then, there would be no "good days!" That is, one has to have some bad days in order to differentiate what is a good day! Like good bounces on the course. If every time I hit a shot, a lucky bounce occurred, believe it or not, soon that would become unexciting & mundane. It takes both good & bad bounces to make the round interesting. Same is true in life.

Jesus told us that in this world there will be tribulation, but be of good cheer, I have overcome the world (John 16:33). A bad bounce followed by a really good bounce! Paul tells us via his word to Timothy that all who live godly in Christ Jesus, shall suffer persecution. (2 Timothy 3:12).

Look at the Book of Job. What a tough read. Bad bounce after bad bounce. That is, until the end of the story. Then we see some really good bounces! But consider what was going on behind the scenes. Things were happening to Job because of variables he had no way of comprehending. A sort of cosmic duel between Satan & God was scripted with Job as the bullet that would hit one of the contestants. Job kept his integrity in not cursing God and in so doing knocked the Accuser off his proverbial block! Job had his moment of greatness because of his trial, because of his bad bounces. Same with Abraham. When God called our father of faith to sacrifice his son Isaac, he didn't know that God was picturing for us three thousand years later what he was planning to do in sacrificing his own beloved Son for us. Abraham didn't know that God would intervene and stop the sacrifice. Talk about a trial, talk about trust & obedience. I sure don't think I could have done that! But that Genesis 22 story was Abraham's greatest moment. And like Job & Abraham, we all will have a few of those chances for greatness during the course of a life. And they always come along side bad bounces. Whether it's sickness or financial crises. Whether it's job distress or natural disaster. How I navigate, how you traverse through that difficulty, determines greatness or mediocrity. Do I trust God, giving him the glory despite my circumstances and thereby become a trophy that God can show off like Job & Abraham, or do I become a little baby complainer, driving people away by my negativity and lack of faith.

You see, when bad bounces happen in life, I still must remember that God is sovereign. He is in control. It's not like God is saying, "Wow, I didn't see that coming." No, he's not surprised when I have a bad bounce in life. In fact, when I read the Book of Job I learn that he allows it! Funny thing really, we all intuitively appreciate the sovereignty of God when it comes to matters in this world that are out of our control, such as, who will be the next President, or protecting us from a falling asteroid. For without his sovereignty, this world would be a scary place indeed. But conversely, we often resent that same sovereignty when it comes to matters that are closer to home, like my health, finances and family. When things don't seem to be smooth in my little kingdom I can resent that same sovereignty of God that I so appreciate on that larger scale. You see my point…that ought not to be. I want to trust him no matter what comes my way. Good bounces or bad. And in the end, when I do, I too, like Job & Abraham, will have a chance for greatness.

For Further Study:

1. When you have a bad bounce on the course what is your response? Can you think of a better way to respond? Even a more fun way to respond?
2. Have you ever had a Job or Abraham moment in life? How did it turn out?
3. Does God's sovereignty comfort you or puzzle you? What would be a good way to respond to his control over your life?

Taking the Low Percentage Shot

The twelfth hole at Eagle Point golf club is one of my favorites. It's a five hundred yard par five, which when played according to the book is a double dog-leg. It lies facing east with the prevailing breeze from behind. Straight on it's about four fifty, but, at the three hundred yard mark is a marsh which protects the green from less than excellent shots. My usual plan for the hole is to hope for a two hundred and thirty or forty yard drive followed by a nice six or seven iron to the left around the side of the marsh and then a gap wedge back the other way to the flag for a one or two putt birdie or par.

But occasionally the wind can be blowing harder or my contact better, and off goes my drive two fifty or two sixty yards. Then I have a dilemma. At one ninety to two hundred yards away, I am tempted to "go for it" with a three-wood or a hybrid. But this is a bad idea, this is called taking the low percentage shot. Nine times out of ten for me, that shot would be lost in the marsh with me taking another ball out of my bag and lying three for the one hundred fifty yard shot over the marsh to the green. All because I was tempted by the possibility of hitting the ball on the green in two and putting for eagle.

In life, taking the low percentage shot can be characterized by the pleasantness of certain sins. For indeed, some sins can be pleasant for a season. Unfortunately, for that man or woman getting a kick out of a certain sin, there will always be a kickback! God's Word is clear on this matter.

For the wages of sin is death.

Romans 6:23

Sin always pays one back with death. Be it death of a relationship or friendship. Death in my mind or health. Death in my job or finances. Sin kills, simple as that. God told his children in the Old Testament that to be sure their sin would find them out, (Jeremiah 2:19). He was saying that it wasn't he who would be doing the correcting but their very sins themselves which would bring about their misery & destruction.

Probably the low percentage shot that is most common to mankind since our earliest days is the sexual sin. Oh, it seems so sweet. The idea of partaking of that forbidden fruit can be overwhelmingly enticing to a man or woman caught in its snare. But afterwards, something always dies. The marriage usually for sure. And of course the collateral damage to the kids cannot be measured. What was so fragrant is always revealed later to be rancid!

> Stolen waters are sweet, and bread eaten in secret is pleasant. But he knoweth not that the dead are there; and that her guests are in the depths of hell.

Proverbs 9:17

Solomon, who knew about sexual sin, states it well when he writes to his son and to us by extension;

> My son, attend unto my wisdom, and bow thine ear to my understanding…For the lips of a strange woman drop as an honeycomb, and her mouth is smoother than oil: But her end is bitter

22

as wormwood, sharp as a two-edged sword. Her
feet go down to death; her steps take hold on
hell…Remove thy way far from her, and come
not nigh to the door of her house. Lest thy give
thine honor unto others, and thy years unto the
cruel: Lest strangers be filled with thy wealth,
and thy labors be in the house of a stranger. And
thou mourn at last when thy flesh and thy body
are consumed.

PROVERBS 5:1, 3-5, 8-11

Sexual sin is pleasant for a season. The lips of that woman or man are indeed sweet. But look what Solomon tells us are its wages. I'll give my honor to others, i.e. embarrassed & humbled. I'll give my years to the cruel, i.e. my life will be shortened. Strangers will take my wealth. Indeed divorce never is a financial positive! And lastly, my flesh & body will be consumed, i.e. disease & premature aging will occur. Without a doubt, sexual sin in life is the golfing equivalent of pulling out that hybrid for the unlikely shot over the marsh.

The low percentage shot is why we need God's Word. For without his Word I really wouldn't know how to handle that strong temptation that life can throw my way.

There is a way which seemeth right unto a man,
but the end thereof are the ways of death.

PROVERBS 14:12

I can't tell on my own what is the right path, God is clear on that truth. I need his direction. In this case, he clearly tells me to stay away from sexual sin. In the New Testament, Paul wrote to Timothy that he was to flee youthful lusts (II Timothy 2:22). Nothing good will come from indulging the flesh in this way.

Thus, as I conclude this comparison of taking the low percentage shot and the pleasantness of certain sins, let me circle back to the beginning. Remember, the proper way to play number twelve at Eagle Point is to go around the marsh, setting up the easy wedge shot for a chance at birdie. Well, lest I think God is a killjoy at keeping me from sexual happiness, let's look at Solomon's conclusion as he describes true sexual intimacy.

> Drink waters out of thine own cistern, and running waters out of thine own well…Let thy fountain be blessed, and rejoice with the wife of thy youth. Let her be as a loving hind and a pleasant roe. Let her breasts satisfy thee at all times and be thou ravished always with her love.
>
> PROVERBS 5:15, 18-19

For Further Study:

1. Can you think of a sin that you haven't regretted yet?
2. What has been your experience in taking the low percentage shot on the course?
3. Can Jesus' sacrifice help you in overcoming sexual sin? See I Corinthians 6:20 for a suggestion. How about II Corinthians 5:14-15 for another helpful thought.

Course Knowledge

Year in and year out my handicap is generally between seven & ten. That's because I have honed it at Centennial golf course in my home town of Medford Oregon. I know the breaks in the green like the back of my hand. I know where to place the drive for optimum results and I know which approach shots are best played aggressively and which ones to back off on. So consequently, I suppose I have a handicap that is lower than if I were playing different golf courses most of the time. When I do get over to Bandon Dunes, Sunriver or Sandpines, most often I'm not hitting or besting my handicap. Pretty easy to know the reason though. I'm not as smart when I play those courses a few times per year. I don't remember about the subtle breaks on the green or how the slope of a certain fairway needs to be accounted for. I forget that the putts don't roll true at slow speed on that oceanside course & I overlook that the wind often plays havoc with a fade on east facing holes at Sandpines turning the shot into a slice.

The term for what I have at Centennial is course knowledge. In life the same thing applies. To negotiate the course of life I need to understand its ways. The place to get that knowledge is found in God's matchless Word. As I study the Bible I obtain the needed skills for living a successful and impacting life. And just as good, if not better, I stand approved by God as I learn to discern truth from error.

> Study to show thyself approved unto God, a workman who needeth not to be ashamed, rightly dividing the word of truth.

II Timothy 2:15

You may remember from the introduction of this book that truth is that which is aligned with the mind, will, character & glory of God. Truth is not what I say it is. (Unless my world-view is that of humanism!) It's what God says it is. That's why I need to have course knowledge of his Word.

Think with me on this, if God says the sky is green, well then, the sky is green! For what God says is, IS. I know that is silly, but extend this thought to our world today to see what I mean. God in the first verse of the Bible says the He created the heavens & the Earth. That's truth, for God said it. So, when professor Doe at Cal Poly says that the Universe & our Earth just happened in the course of evolution. That's error, that's not true. Or when God proclaims in the Psalms that he knew us before we were born & that we were fearfully and wonderfully made in our mother's womb, that's truth. So, when the Supreme Court holds that it's okay to snuff out that same life in the womb, because it's not really a person yet. That's false, that's wrong. It's God's Word that gives me the needed perspective, the proper world-view so that I can discern truth from error.

I alluded to Humanism above. This is one of the major religions in America & the Western world. It's the world-view that I am at the center of things. It's the arrogant belief that I am a little god, if you will. Truth is relative in the humanistic thought and there are no absolutes. Obviously, humanistic thought has no place for God & his Word. "Thus saith the Lord" doesn't fly for the humanist!

The second major American false religion is closely related. It is called Pluralism. This is the belief that all religions are correct. It too is an arrogant religion in itself, rejecting all others as being inferior, especially Christianity. To the Pluralist, Christians are intolerant and haters, sticking to their absolutes that God in his Word declares to them. But of course, Pluralism has a fatal flaw. If all religions are equally true, (Islam, Hinduism, New Age philosophy etc.) then by extension, since they do not teach the same things, they are equally false! And the "tolerance" they preach is similarly inconsistent. The "New Tolerance" they expound says I must approve of and agree with everyone. It doesn't matter if what they say is diametrically opposed to each other! But, since they have no absolutes, I guess they can twist their logic to get to this otherwise illogical conclusion. On the other hand, the "True Tolerance" that I feel the Bible teaches, and what I want in my life, says that I should give people the freedom of their world-view even when I don't approve or agree with it. True tolerance refuses to hate, but loves! What it doesn't do, is throw truth out the window. It marries grace & truth. I will love you no matter what, but I won't accept what you say if it goes against what my God has clearly stated. I'm going to rightly divide the Word. I want to stand approved before my Maker. I'm going to pursue life's course knowledge.

For Further Study:

1. Do you think about where the pin is placed on the green before you hit your second shot on a par 5?
2. Do you believe in the "New Tolerance" that all roads lead to God? Why or why not?
3. How can you be truly tolerant yet stand for truth in your workplace, at home, on the golf course?

Iron Sharpens Iron

Golf is a social game. It is meant to be enjoyed with friends as we share the bond of athletics. But it is also a competitive game. Therein lies a problem. For the competition should be against myself and the course and not against my playing partners. So often I forget this fact and start comparing myself to my playing partner. If he is playing well it can bring me down into a funk of self-defeat whereas if she is having a bad day I may feel prideful in my superior ability. Obviously, neither place is where I want to go.

Both of these comparative states have parallels to my spiritual walk. When I relate myself to my Pastor or to brothers who seem to have their spiritual lives dialed in, I can feel pretty low about myself. Whereas, when I look at folks whose lives are a mess, I can get pretty smug and complacent in my mind. Both, of course, are bad. My only comparison in life should be to my Lord. He is the standard. He is the one who is typified as the golf course itself.

When I'm out playing a round, my focus should be on playing against the course and my previous self (i.e. my handicap) and not looking to better my playing partner. You see, Jesus is the golf course. He sets the bar, not other people. He is perfect and I want to be like him, understanding that in this life, that goal is unattainable. That would be like shooting birdie on every hole. Like getting a 54. Just not going to happen. But as I go against the course, making that my aim, I can be much more satisfied after my round than when I compare myself to others.

We have a promise from God's Word that we can look to when we compare ourselves to Jesus and our future hope.

> Beloved, now are we the sons of God, and it doth not yet appear what we shall be: But we know that, when he shall appear, we shall be like him; for we shall see him as he is. And every man that hath this hope in him purifieth himself, even as he is pure.
>
> I JOHN 3:2-3

Now we see dimly, we are told in 1ˢᵗ Corinthians 13:12, but then face to face. On that future day we will see clearly. So, as I play the course, and not my golfing buddy, I get the spiritual equivalent of looking to Jesus, who is the author and finisher of my faith.

Now don't get me wrong, it's fine to play little golf games with your friends, like match play, total score, etc., but the focus still needs to be on playing the course and your previous self, not the other guy or gal. It's like that video game you have at home, playing in the self only mode, where you compete against your previous scores. That's how I want to compete on the course too. When I do that I am much more satisfied after the round. I suspect you will be also.

But extending this idea further. Since I know that I have this natural tendency to go up against the other guy instead of just playing the course, it's important that I play with players of similar ability. Once again, when I'm playing with that "scratch" golfer, my flesh drives me to swing too hard and otherwise mess up and get down on myself. Contrastingly, when I'm joined up with the proverbial "hacker," then boastful arrogance can creep into my mind. But, when golfing with players of my level, we can actually feed off of each other and sometimes the flow back & forth between our shots can become magical as we both occasionally get into the groove and play better because of our similar skill sets.

In spiritual life this is how brothers & sisters in the Lord help each other out.

> Iron sharpens iron; so a man sharpeneth the countenance of his friend.
>
> PROVERBS 27:17

I want to spend time with some brothers who are going to sharpen my walk with Jesus by building me up, by holding me accountable to my commitments and towards holiness itself, and by sharing God's Word with me as we talk about the stuff of our lives. So, I want to surround myself with guys who will do that. Pray with them, golf with them, fellowship with them. I don't want to spend quality time, and golfing is quality time, around negative, godless men and women who aren't going to sharpen my soul & to whom I'm unable to pour out treasure that God has given me. It just a waste of an otherwise good day and a good round!

For Further Study:

1. Do you have a favorite golfing partner? Why is he or she your favorite?
2. How can you maximize your time together on the course to walk away the better after a round of golf?
3. What qualities do you see in Jesus that you would like to have exhibited in your life?

Trusting the Line

All golfers have had this happen to them. Standing over a putt which you "know" breaks left but your playing partner just struck nearly the same putt from a few feet further away and it broke right. What do you do? Do you believe what you feel or do you trust what you just saw happen to his ball as likely going to happen to yours also? This is called trusting the line and it's important because as a golfer stands over a putt at a ninety degree angle from the cup the visual often is different than what he saw in his walk around or from observing other shots on the green. Thus, it is critically important to commit to the line from your observations & your walk around and then strike the putt with confidence trusting the line and not your faulty senses of the moment.

In life, same thing is in play. Will I walk by faith, trusting the line of God's Word or will I follow hard after my fleshly five senses? Paul tells us that we find success in life as we walk by faith and not by sight (II Corinthians 5:7). We can and often are fooled by our senses. Thinking for instance, that something is going to be bad, only later to find out that it turned out very well. God tells me to walk by faith in what he says is true. He tells me that all things will work together for good in my life (Romans 8:28). That doesn't mean that everything will be good but that everything will mix together and with God's amazing redemptive ability, he will turn things destined to be bad, to good. An illness or job setback will come along seemingly out of the blue and be very distressing. I want to complain and become negative but walking by faith frees me from this. Maybe the Lord will use that illness or disappointment to minister to that nurse caring for me or redirect me to that new location he desires for me. Just no way for me to tell. Thus, I need to trust him.

You know, this concept really exposes the fallacy of the paradigm that many people hold onto which says that the world and the events of our lives are governed by mere chance. You see, what we know of our world and even of our very lives is only the tip of the iceberg. There are far too many mysteries which are not at all comprehended by me, by us, by mankind. Living by faith and not needing to "figure" everything out is the way I want to live. Thus, I must direct you again to one of my favorites.

> Therefore, being justified by faith, we have peace
> with God through our Lord Jesus Christ.
>
> Romans 5:1

If I want to have peace, then God in his Word tells me it's by faith in Jesus Christ, not by my vast knowledge or experience that will deliver on that promise. Walking by faith in God is the way to live. It's a cool breeze, it's a warm day in April, it's trusting the line for success in golf & in life.

For Further Study:

1. Are putts breaking to the left or the right harder for you to read correctly?
2. On breaking putts, do you most often miss high or low?
3. You are saved by grace through faith (Ephesians 2:6). How does that translate over to your daily walk? See Colossians 2:6.

Preparation

Which is better? To rush over to the course after a prior commitment barely making my tee time & causing my buddies to wait for me, or getting to the course forty five minutes prior to my start time giving me some time to take some practice putts and swings? Well, the latter of course. Giving myself time to focus on my upcoming round sets me up for success just as failing to prepare mentally & physically before my round sets me up for failure.

Same is true for my day-to-day life. I need to leave for work by 7:30 most days. Now, I can wake up giving myself just enough time to shower, dress & rush to the car or I can get up a little earlier and enjoy a nice cup of coffee spending time with my Lord in fellowship, prayer and reading his Word. Again, it's the latter choice that sets my day up for success!

> Thy word have I hid in my heart, that I might not
> sin against thee.
>
> PSALM 119:11

This verse I have memorized. For as I hide the Word in my heart, as I memorize chunks of scripture, I feed the "saint" in me, not the "sinner!" Over and over in the scripture, God tells us to meditate on his Word. (Joshua 1:8 & Psalm 1:1-3 among others.) But it takes discipline to do this. My fleshly mind wants to sleep in. Thus, I must decide that I'm going to prepare for the day. As I do, I will be rewarded with good success. As I meet with Jesus in the morning, it makes me happy as I feel his touch, get direction for the day and leave for work ready to bless others with the love and fellowship I've just had with my Savior.

> Cause me to hear thy lovingkindness in the morning; for in thee do I trust: Cause me to know the way wherein I should walk; for I lift my soul unto thee.
>
> PSALM 143:8

This is my prayer every morning.

Jesus believed this approach to life also. The Bible states that he would wake up before the dawn of the day to spend time with his Father. Well, if the Sun of Righteousness had to get his spiritual batteries recharged every morning, certainly you & I do even so much more!

> The Lord God hath given me the tongue of the learned, that I should know how to speak a word in season to him that is weary: He wakeneth morning by morning, he wakeneth mine ear to hear as the learned.
>
> ISAIAH 50:4

If I want to help people, and I do. If I want to make a difference, and I do, then I must prepare. And the best thing about the discipline of preparation is that it is not onerous. It has become one of the joys of my life being able to get up to the sun and spend time with the Son!

Indeed, preparation is important, both in golf before each round and in life before each day.

For Further Study:

1. Do you have a routine that you like to do prior to each round?
2. Have you memorized any Bible verses? Try high-lighting some in your Bible or on your Bible App & practice them for a couple of minutes in the morning.
3. Think of a time God gave you a word to speak to the weary. Would it have helped if it actually were a Bible verse? As has been said, speaking the scriptures is like letting a lion out of his cage!

Practice

Practice is important. And it also can and should be fun. As I work on my swing, concentrating on the sum of the parts I can improve my game while at the same time build muscle memory for use later out on the course. For on the course, I don't really want to be concentrating on the sum of the parts at all. There, I want to go with the flow of the swing, with only one or two swing thoughts in my mind. Things like we've discussed before, e.g., keep your eye on the ball or swing easy, staying in balance.

Besides frequent, if not daily practice, it's also important to vary my practice. One day I might focus on full swings where another should be devoted to chipping, putting or sand play. If I always work on full swings but never practice the short game or putting, I may have good ball striking ability but still shoot a poor score as I struggle on & around the greens.

Same is true in spiritual life. The equivalent of practice in golf is reading the Bible & prayer. When I read the Word of God I hear his heart on matters of the heart as well as see his Son on most every page. As I pray, I release my worries & concerns, freeing up my mind from life's clutter that can so easily bog me down. A little limerick that I often whisper to myself concerning this spiritual practice goes like this…Read my Bible & pray, every single day!

On the driving range, it's important to recreate conditions that may come up in a round. That is, instead of just blasting mindlessly, I want to think about the shots, maybe aim at certain targets or try to shape my ball flight. Things that could come up later on the course. On the green, I need to practice breakers both ways as well as up & downhill putts and ones with and against the grain of the green.

In my spiritual practice, reading the Word conversationally is my recommendation. That is, as I'm reading scripture, I frequently want to stop and talk to the Lord about what I'm sensing, tell him if I don't understand something or praise him for how outrageously wonderful something else is that I come across. It's like talking to a good friend. The conversation is not one sided where he talks, then stops & then I talk. No, we both interject talking from one to the other so that our interaction is free flowing and fun, not stiff and regimented.

Another important thing about practice is that I want to do it correctly. If I'm practicing my swing using poor technique, well, that's not going to be good. In that case, I will just hone my muscle memory to include the various swing flaws that I always practice. Of course, my swing isn't ever going to be like Jordan Spieth's or Jason Day's, but it should build upon swing principles consistent with a man of my age, strength and overall flexibility.

Likewise, in my spiritual practice time with the Lord, as I read his Word and talk conversationally with him, I need to be ready to do what I learn & hear from him. If I'm not willing to do what he clearly tells me to do, ultimately my close walk with him will suffer as I drift slowly away not realizing that I'm missing out on what he has for me. His ways for me are always good. It's only because of my frequent lack of trust in him that I can miss out.

Couple of verses come to mind to illustrate this principle. There are many more of course.

> For I know the thoughts that I think toward you,
> saith the Lord, thoughts of peace, and not of evil,
> to give you an expected end.

JEREMIAH 29:11

Truly our God can be trusted to always have our best interests at heart.

Jehovah's commission to Joshua is appropriate to this discussion.

> This book of the law shall not depart out of thy
> mouth; but thou shalt meditate therein day and
> night, that thou mayest observe to do according
> to all that is written therein: For then thou shalt
> make thy way prosperous, and then thou shalt
> have good success.

JOSHUA 1:8

As I do the words that I receive from the One who gave it all for me, not just mentally agree, but actually do the words, then I have good success. Just like practicing golf is better for my game than just watching it on TV, so too, is doing the word better than just agreeing with it.

For Further Study:

1. What do you like best about golf practice?
2. Do you think God is bothered by tough questions?
3. Can you think times when you did & did not do what you clearly heard the Lord tell you to do from his Word? How did those times work out?

Playing By the Rules

Rules are important. Both in golf and for navigating a successful life. By definition, any game I play, whether it be poker or baseball, whether it be scrabble or shuffleboard, whether it be best ball or the game of life, all are governed by its game's particular rules. When I do not follow those rules, well I'm playing a different game.

Am I golfing if I hit three Mulligans per nine, move my ball forward out of the hazard without penalty & bump my ball out of the edge of the rough on a routine basis? Many weekend players indulge these indiscretions most every round. Does it matter? The answer to me is…it depends! If I play with my friends and we all agree that these "winter" rules are applicable, well then maybe it's okay. After all, we're playing to have fun, relax and get some exercise over trying to compete for the professional tour. But certainly, I don't want to be keeping score if I'm playing with this loosy-goosy mind set, and definitely I should not be turning in my score for handicap purposes.

You see, it does matter if I plan to play under the handicap system, as my USGA official handicap levels the playing field to a great degree. It's much like proper tee selection helps the short-hitter enjoy a round with the bomber. But handicaps are only as good as the integrity by which they are kept. Adding and subtracting shots, called sandbagging & revising take away from the handicap system greatly. Really it is all about integrity. It's about my willingness to be truthful about my ability on the course. If I can't do that, then I should just play for the joy of the game and not worry about my score.

Now one may say, I want to play by the rules, but I don't like all of them. Why should I have to take stroke & distance when hitting out-of-bounds? Why not just a stroke with a lateral shot from the nearest relief? Or why must I play the ball from the divot it just rolled into? Seems sort of unfair, I'll just bump the ball a bit. Well the answer to these questions which seem to come up in every round is, I (you) didn't make the rules. But if we want to play golf, well then we must follow them or we are playing something else.

Same is true in life. We didn't make the rules, God did. But if I want to live life with integrity, then I should follow the rules He has set up. The world-view that I can do whatever I want as long as it doesn't affect someone else is just as flawed as the golfing examples given above.

The Lord has given us rules out of love, not out of a mean spirit. He's not a cosmic killjoy wanting to suppress my happiness, for he knows ultimately, as I follow the rules he has given, I will be the happier for it.

But rules, won't love me! Only a relationship with him can do that. In fact, it's the very rules of life which he has given me, which I fail to keep on regular basis, that reveal to me that I need a relationship with him. Paul stated this idea with these words found in Galatians.

> Wherefore the law was our schoolmaster to bring
> us unto Christ, that we might be justified by faith.
> But after faith is come, we are no longer under
> a schoolmaster.

GALATIANS 3:24-25

You see, it's the rules God has given in his Word which reveal to you and me that we need a Savior. For we can't keep them. The temptation to break the rules is just too great! But when faith came, we are no longer under the schoolmaster. Now, by faith in Christ, declaring him to be my Lord & Redeemer, I can live free in a relationship, and not be bound by the rules that I couldn't keep. Now I can go out and have fun playing the game I enjoy without keeping score.

But even though I've been set free from the law of sin & death (Romans 8:2), I still don't want to go out and willfully sin. For sin has repercussions. Yes, when I sin, I'm still saved, but I will suffer the consequences of my bad choices. The Bible says "be sure, your sin will find you out!" God doesn't slam me when I sin, it's my own sin that boomerangs back and wipes me out.

> Thine own wickedness shall correct thee, and thy backslidings shall reprove thee.
>
> JEREMIAH 2:19

So I want to live holy. I want to follow the rules. I want to keep score! As had been oft said, holiness equals happiness!

> Who among us will dwell with the devouring fire? Who among us will dwell with everlasting burnings? He that walketh righteously, and speaketh uprightly: He that despiseth the gain of oppressions, that shaketh his hands from holding of bribes, that stoppeth his ears from hearing of blood, and shutteth his eyes from seeing evil: He shall dwell on high.
>
> ISAIAH 33:14-16

For Further Study:

1. How's your handicap? Is it solid, sandbagging or revising? Does it matter?
2. Are God's commands important to follow? Are you a spirit or a letter of the law person?
3. Does your faith in the Lord give you freedom to do whatever?

Helping a Friend Find His Lost Ball

I'm on the 5th tee with my friend Greg. It's a beautiful autumn day in Medford Oregon with cool breezes and warm sunshine blessing us on our round at Centennial Golf Course. We both parred number four but I have the honors from the third hole and hit a nice drive just to the right of the three traps that guard against trying to cut the corner on this short dogleg left hole. Greg is up next & he too doesn't want to hit into one of the sand traps, but unfortunately for him, he overcompensates a little too much sending his drive into some tall weeds & brush which grew up over the summer on the right of the fairway and adjacent rough. Thus, he has lost his ball & would like to find it.

Well, I can say "tough luck old buddy" and casually walk up to my shot or I can do the right thing and help him find his ball. He's going to appreciate it much if I aid him and probably be a bit annoyed if I just check out, forgetting that he is in some trouble on the course.

Same is true in my day-to-day life. The Bible tells me that we are to bear one another's burdens, (Galatians 6:2). We are to help out, to lift up, to support that friend, co-worker, brother or sister when they are in need. You know, the Golden Rule: Do unto others…

When Jesus was asked, what is the greatest commandment in the Law, how did he respond?

Thou shalt love the Lord thy God with all thy heart, and with all thy soul, and with all thy mind. This is the first and great commandment. And the second is like unto it, thou shalt love thy neighbor as thyself. On these two commandments hang all the law and the prophets.

MATTHEW 22:37-40

The Bible says love covers a multitude of sins (1 Peter 4:8). Of the three things that endure, faith, hope & love, love is the greatest! (I Corinthians 13:13) Conversely, without love, I'm really not much of a friend. I'm just a "taker" & not a "giver." I want to be a friend. One of my favorite proverbs speaks to friendship, to bearing one another's burdens;

He who hath friends must show himself friendly.

PROVERBS 18:24

Helping a friend find his ball, bearing one another's burdens, takes work. It breaks the flow of my game, it can be a distraction in my daily game of life. But the paradox is, that work, like exercise, is at first hard, but then the second wind kicks in. I get that good feeling that comes from extending myself instead of just living for myself and my own little world! Jesus of course, said it best, "For whosoever will save his life shall lose it, but whosoever will lose his life for my sake, the same shall save it" (Luke 9:24).

As I help my friend find his ball, I will be the better for it. As we bear one another's burdens, we will be living like our Lord did. I'll take that over a good drive any day!

For Further Study:

1. Do you watch your playing partner's shots?
2. Which is better, speaking with the tongues of men or of angels or having love? Playing excellent golf or being a good friend?
3. Which is easier, living for your agenda or another's? Which is best?

Finding a Friend's Lost Ball

It was a Pro V1 that Greg lost. Those popular balls that many use believing they will enhance their distance on the fairway and their ball control around the green. Yet Pro V1's are expensive! Around four bucks per ball, forty eight big ones for a box of twelve. So, losing a Pro V1 is not the same as misplacing some lessor brand! So we want to find it, even if it takes a little time.

So we looked for a couple of minutes…and you know what happened next. The group behind us walked off the last green and came up to the tee getting ready to hit. Unfortunately, we were still within their reach and thus they needed to wait! So, reluctantly we gave up and Greg pulled out another ball to hit.

Next, something wonderful happened. After he played another shot we got in the cart and drove up another thirty yards towards the green where we spotted Greg's ball right next to the cart path! What joy, we found the lost ball!

Jesus spoke of joy infinitely greater when he told us of the joy in heaven when a shepherd finds his lost little lamb.

> What man of you, having a hundred sheep, if he lose one of them, doth not leave the ninety nine and go after that which was lost? And when he hath found it, he lays it on his shoulder rejoicing. And when he comes home, he calls together his friends saying rejoice with me for I have found

my sheep which was lost. I say unto you, that
likewise joy shall be in heaven over one sinner
that repents.

LUKE 15:4-7

I don't think about heaven enough! It sounds really great.
One of the best things about it will be the incredible joy that will
be there. How good it is to remind ourselves frequently of the
wonderful hope we have waiting for us in heaven with our Lord.

Eye hath not seen, nor ear heard, neither have
entered into the heart of man, the things which
God hath prepared for them that love him,

1 CORINTHIANS 2:21

I think of a baby every time I consider this verse. Specifically
the fetus in mother's womb. It's dark, he's never been in the
light. He doesn't understand poetry, science or really anything
about this world. Yet, he is nonetheless born into the light and
acclimates over time just like we will when we are "born into
the light." The parallel is true. I was born once & I will be born
again…again!

In my Father's house are many mansions. If it
were not so, I would have told you. I go to prepare a place for you. And if I go and prepare
a place for you, I will come again, and receive
you unto myself; that where I am, there ye may
be also.

JOHN 14: 2-3

What a promise. Just as Jesus came to earth the first time. A historical fact. So too, he will come again. This is the hope of heaven that keeps me going when life gets a little tough. John tells me that this hope of seeing Jesus is what purifies my heart as I seek to finish strong in this life.

> But we know that, when he shall appear, we shall be like him. For we shall see him as he is. And every man that hath this hope in him purifieth himself, even as he is pure.
>
> I JOHN 3:2-3

"Now the God of hope fill you with all joy & peace in believing" (Rom 15:13).

Indeed, the joy of finding that lost ball is but a glimpse of the joy waiting for us when we find the object of all of our desires, when we see our Lord face to face!

For Further Study:

1. Are happiness & joy the same? Why or why not?
2. There are parallels between a fetus in the womb & our lives here on Earth. Can you think of some parallels between the birth of a baby & our deaths?
3. Do you have proof that Jesus' first coming was an historical fact?

The Sandie

Everyone loves the underdog. We often find ourselves rooting for the team whom the odds makers say is going to lose. We read books and go to movies expecting to experience some twists and turns in the story and we love it when the hero comes out of difficult circumstances for that happy ending. This is why all golfers note the "sandie" when it occurs. For it truly is a reflection of the life we all long for.

Bobby and I are on the eighteenth hole in our little game of match play. It's all tied up and we both hit good tee shots leaving us one hundred & seventy yards to the green. Bobby, using a long iron, makes a beautiful shot leaving him thirty feet away from the cup for a relatively easy two putt and a par. But I'm not so fortunate. I need to use a hybrid club, but my shot drifts slightly to the right and into the sand trap guarding the right side of the green on this long par four hole. I'm in trouble and it's looking bad. Golfers watching would agree that I'm the underdog and place their bets on Bobby to win the match and enjoy all the bragging rights that accompany his victory.

But then the unexpected happens. Using my sand wedge I execute the shot of the round for me as my ball floats toward the cup stopping six inches from the cup for a tap in par. Bobby, of course, predictably two putts and we both walk away feeling good about our round and the game. He, as expected, has a comment or two about my lucky shot, but it is all in good fun.

So it is in life. We were all in the trap. We were like that ball which landed near the top of the trap and plugged, fried egg style, in the sand. Getting up and down in two in the game of life didn't look good.

But then we were given a second chance. After the bad shot in life that put us in the trap, for that's what our sin did, Jesus gave us a second chance at par.

For Jesus came to earth on that Christmas morning, lived the life God intended for Adam & all of us to live, and then he went to the Cross as our substitute, as our Redeemer! He paid the price for our sin & stupidity and God ratified his sacrifice by raising him from the dead. Now, all that is required is that we put our faith in him. That is, we must execute the sand shot!

> For God so loved the world, that he gave his only son, that whosoever believes in him shall not perish but have everlasting life.
>
> JOHN 3:16

You see, in the game of life, we were originally under the Law. Humanity was given the opportunity to live life according to God's standards. Unfortunately, none of us could do that. Not Bobby or me, not Adam or you! "For all have sinned and fall short of the glory of God" (Romans 3:23).

But then faith came. And not faith in faith, but faith in Jesus. As we believe in him, as the Bible's most famous verse declares we gain everlasting life. You see, faith is the sandie. It's the second chance. It's the underdog we are all rooting for! Faith in Jesus is what brings life to your soul.

> Whosoever believeth that Jesus is the Christ is born of God...For whatsoever is born of God

overcomes the world: And this is the victory that overcometh the world, even our faith.

I JOHN 5:1 & 4

Faith is the victory (Greek; nike) that overcomes the world. And it's the underdog. We didn't see it coming at all. We thought we had to work for our salvation. But we don't! No hoops to jump through. No race to win. All we need to do is take the shot!

Faith is not fantasy or wishful thinking. God says faith is what makes me victorious. Jesus said to Thomas, that wonderful doubting disciple who is like so many of us, "blessed are they that have not seen, and yet have believed" (John 20:29). How awesome is that statement! It warms my heart. We have not seen him. Yet we believe. Jesus says we are blessed!

And faith in God is rational based upon so much evidence from his past dealings with us. That is, we see the world around us that he created. We understand that he came the first time into our world as an irrefutable historical fact and thus by faith we extend the belief that he will do what he says he will do in the future. That is, save us and take us to heaven to be with him forever!

Oh, how I thank God for faith in Jesus Christ. It's the greatest sandie of all time!

For Further Study:

1. Match play or total score. Which game do you like better when competing? Why?
2. Are people inherently good or bad? Can you support your world view of this biblically?
3. Can God be trusted to do what he says in regards to your future? What evidence do you have from his past dealings with you?

Epilogue

So we come to the end of this book. We've seen parallels with discipline, integrity, fellowship & truth that are imbedded in the game of golf that we can carry over to successful living of our day to day lives. I hope you have enjoyed this little look at life the way God intended us to live it as we've looked through the lens of golf. Now go out there and play well…and go forth & live well!

About the Author

Daniel Tomlinson grew up around golf and has enjoyed the game for decades. He has published three other books which are available at vendors worldwide. Daniel lives in Northwest Montana on Flathead Lake with his wife Julie and their four dogs.

Acknowledgements

Special thanks to my good golfing buddy Greg Knudson. On many enjoyable rounds together we would fellowship around the Lord & golf. Our frequent discussions about the many parallels between good golf and a successful life were the catalyst in writing this book.

Milton Keynes UK
Ingram Content Group UK Ltd.
UKHW021813260124
436770UK00010B/692